DIALECTIC
BY
SAM R GERAGHTY

All rights reserved, no part of this publication may be either reproduced or transmitted by any means whatsoever without the prior permission of the publisher.

VENEFICIA PUBLICATIONS UK

Editing & Typesetting © Veneficia Publications UK
September 2019

Cover image © Gavyn Dylan Sodo
Facebook/BlackInkVoid

CONTENTS

DOUBT ... 1
INTRO ... 2
TRICK OF THE LIGHT ...3
SON OF MARY ... 4
KNIGHT ... 5
MASK ... 6
MITHRIDATES VI ... 7

RUMINATION ... 9
INTRO ... 10
ROAD TO URUK ... 11
BREATHE ... 13
SHADOW ... 14
IMMOLATION ... 15
THE VESSEL ... 16

REVELATION ... 17
INTRO ... 18
REVELATION ... 19
DESCENT ... 20
MONOLITH ... 23
EPITAPH ... 25
LIQUID ... 26

IMMORTAL ... 27

ECSTASY ... 28
INTRO ... 29
EVE ... 30
AMOR ... 31
BELTAIN ... 32
DEATH OF ADONIS ... 33
INCITER ... 34
MAENAD ... 35
SUCCUBUS ... 36

ADORATION ... 37
INTRO ... 38
SONG-FATHER ... 39
APHRODITE ... 40
TO ORPHEUS ... 42
PERSEPHONE ... 43
THE HAG OF LOCH BA ... 44
CIRCE ... 45
DREAM ... 47

INTRODUCTION

Poetry is a lost Art.

We live in a world where everything must be cut into bite sized pieces for people to ingest, for people to find palatable.

Everything is go, go, go in this technological world where information that cannot fit onto a meme is simply discarded and not absorbed by the vast majority of people.

This translates over to the writing world where Social Media has given everyone the power to "be a writer," and it's a place that is saturated with one-liners that are passed off as Poetry.

Bite sized Poetry.

We all have our own tastes, but for me, Poetry is to be savored; a taste that lingers in your mouth long after the words have gone, like the kiss of a lover.
It's supposed to be painful, powerful and full of Plutonian energy.

Pain can be both beautiful and ugly; so, too, can Pluto.

Poets are a breed of their own, in a world of their own, telling stories of the human condition in a way that others simply don't see it.

Sam is one of those rare, rare Poets.

I thought the days of Great Poets were long gone; I would chalk it up to changing times, but then I met a beautiful Aquarian Soul, a Rebel Sage and his words changed my life.

He will tell you how I changed his life, that I gave him a chance and believed in him when no one else did; some of that may be true, but Sam's words saved me.

His presence in my life has saved me.

This book has saved me.

Poetry is meant to be felt, but it's also meant to be read out loud at your own pace, and that is what I encourage you to do with this book.

Let it touch your Soul, let it drudge up those dark feelings, let it heal you.

With each poem, I found myself, and my Soul take a sigh of relief; some poems made me laugh, some made me cry, and there was a poem or two that sent me down a rabbit hole in search of historical context.

Is that not what good--no, no, great writing is supposed to do? Make you want more? Make you search for more?!

That is precisely what this book does.

This book is exquisite rebellion presented in a way that the reader will be different just from reading it once; I have read four times, and there are a few poems I have read countless times.

Humanity has lost touch with the Arts, and Arts Programs are being stripped out of our schools; given our current social and political climates being at all time tension highs, we need Artistic expression NOW more than ever.

Art, in any form, is about many things, but it's primarily about making the viewer/reader FEEL something.

Allow the word Alchemy that Sam gifts you with on these pages to feel something.

After all, that is what Great Poetry is supposed to do.

That is what Great Art is supposed to do, and this book is Art.

JACLYN CHERIE

DOUBT

*The sea retreats,
the moon tilts back on herself
as the purple sky embraces of the still...
even hope turns back
her murmurs on the breeze
for the song was sung so sadly...*

TRICK OF THE LIGHT

The silent moon peeks
from behind innocent clouds,

like a murderess
that loiters in night's temple.

She strikes wildly,
eerie in her vindictiveness

she is the hangman,
passing a virgin
to the mouth of a wolf.

She laughs at the tears
shed in her name,

blesses the saliva
borne of crooked teeth

whilst other celestial guests
refrain,

till the light dims out;
the universe to vanish
and play no more of her game.

SON OF MARY

I watch, stranded in the freeze, immovable;
there is nothing but my pondering silence.

I hoped once hope would bring forth life!
But the rivers that flow run rich with sorrow

and only the forests will hear my lament
as I sing to my own deep well.

So profound is my grief, I wander an exile;
a creature whom love abandoned;

as a wolf on the steppes whose hunger never ceased.

KNIGHT

You
mirror in the vault,
clown at the grail

nursling monster just begun –
raw beast
whom shuns at every stage the march of the light
like some calamity
dancing destitute the chime.

Twisted root, rotten trunk
a branch of the dead –
he said:

'Now hold out your hand and receive me...
I am your degenerate
my ashen face, eternal -
atrocious as death in your heart,
my lag...
in the cadaver of the moment
you bleed in your flesh sack,
then die again...

again.

To bury the poxy nag of the fallen self -
stunted
shining
to revel
noxious as the ray,
sullied as the waning moon
waiting on the glory
of the Knight
turned day.

MASK

From the nest to depart
you were harried from the husk which gave origin
to spread as far as the punctured light would flee;
to inhabit
mesmerize
possess
the dead among the living...

Your swindled word disintegrates
no marble weeps in your name,
disguised no more in my shuddering dream,
your fraud wanders on, aloof
bereft of any anchor, swept along
in the maddening breath...

MITHRIDATES VI

Toward the unknown,
swathed in the cloak of unforgiving time
audacious I defy in advance.

I am Mithra's gift and I seek
to hammer darkness
down upon your light.

I will tear down your Venus!
Only your Jove will remain
my father of the lightning.

If this is your light
Rome, we gave you our sun -
it is all you understand.

I speak the tongue
he is brother
I have drunk of the poison,

he is brother
but I have better form than this gutless parade
more spine, for I am crueller than he,
I twist my knives.

They will send me Pompey some day
no doubt ruined then I shall be
the King of Pontus, forced
to work on some second-rate snot;
in the meanwhile
I am on your frontier come the dawn

Dear Senate, I am meteor
destined -
I wish only End in blood-forge

Luperca's milk will run dry
no legion can steady this course -
this is eternal.

I am Mithra's gift and I seek
to hammer darkness
down upon your light.

I will tear down your Venus!
Only your Jove will remain
my father of the lightning

I am poison –
lantern of the Black sea,
Mithradates!
long my ghost may savage you, Rome
in the last vestiges of your hour.

RUMINATION

*Lush rebel of unbroken promise -
feast no more on silence,
complicit. Civilization is
he who will not venture
beyond the rugged scarp
nor drink of the deathless vine,
to bathe in the lake of liberty
unfettered, unreasoned...*

ROAD TO URUK

I hear you
like a mirror would
I can see you gasp...

your ripple was sent
downstream into deep intention
many loves ago
beyond the reckoning of age.

It is our story
we common hearts once did beat
to the skin-drums of the animal Gods
on the road to Uruk.

Order may collapse,
war may ransack the heart,
shattering the brief architecture,

levelling all that is solid
back into air
laying waste our divine huts,
overcoming the crumbling foundation.

The structure lasts as long as it takes
pre-eminence to elude the city-state
when the hunter becomes his prey
in constant metamorphosis;

city of the cosmos –
a rite of initiation
held within the holy gates of void
and discord.

To dream of Mesopotamia,
of elements won

stock of toil and innovation
this never-ending struggle -
first parent city
of civilization shine!

And the Gods...
they will retreat
behind a human mask –

we must work their art
ride the venture of the chaos
kiss the flux
incipient and grand;
do we trust in the hand?

You that took the torch,
brutal pioneer
who wrestled with fate and the Earth

Seven millennia on,
Ishtar is dressed again
at the first of seven gates...

Now the key to the soul is found
beneath the unnatural hooves
of our road
into the gutter and the glory
along the many crooked crossroads

toward a new Babylon.

BREATHE

I come as form -
like a cone imparting whirlwind
motion as God
I am manifest
here
I move like the clouds...

Drunk on the vital poison
I breathe the corporeal
delirium flown as a dove of heaven
and the cunning of the Earth's lost serpent
with the heart of a changeling,
present at each of many deaths...

Before I go again into the solitude,
into that place where all poets thrive
in the solitary beat of the heart
I breathe in all creation...

...and you will know by now the end of the tale
as I breathe in,
I must exhale.

SHADOW

The eye of the dream has no face
and yet I know its intent...
there alongside the chirr of my heart,
I summon untold story seep within,
where it shall flow, a river of uncertainty
through the jilted mind
like a ghost in the stream...

I grip each rung of my lone cavort -
banish fear
welcome the runt of my own yesteryear
as much as it takes me to grasp;
that the vault houses unchained memory
and here the phantoms unleashed scratch in the dark
to be heard, blessed voice, graced
with charmed mirror,
like virgins to the sun they will bask
unified when the battle is won
in the god-flesh of my untold fear.

IMMOLATION

Speak through me...
the ash on hearth is stone-cold
and I burn to tell...

Of the soul caged behind closed door;
to rot dank unlit, yet fed, clothed and watered.
Bled from the womb in a pogrom of the self,
engulfed in corridors of knowing.

My martyred mind is thrown to the pyre
but wings spread graceful their departure...

I left
with my brother - Doubt,
or maybe I am not supposed to remember
such things?

Once word had sprung,
both of us scarpered from the throat
and the only token I own
is the glory beheld
on the steel tip
of an arrow that breached.

VESSEL

'I am sadness' says the old man to the sea -
Where underneath an autumn moon
He stares at his own melancholy solitude
Bids the woeful tide come home
As he turns away the stranger to his grief;
For water will always mock a faltering fire
And wretched fail the embers in their dusk
As if his passion was but curse...

He turns the other cheek, his vessel full to brim
With salt-tears comes that darker wine he drinks;
That same wine bestows his blissful child
A deeper peace within.

REVELATION

*Beautiful night, embrace me
within your cradle of silence
whereupon the ancient winds
abide among the oldest trees,
till the murmurs softly speak
between our distant time...*

REVELATION

It is my enduring love of the dark
Which bade me glimpse behind the drape.
That moment before the sun doth set
Deep in the crimson sky, this shroud -
My herald, emerge to walk of the Earth!
Where I have wallowed many thousands of years
In my legitimacy, deserted though my soul -
A vessel, mere husk I drink the last mile
Before the fury of the dawn, I am eternity!
And I have become of the great pulse of life...

DESCENT

Like a star that struck its chord...

I am sent downstream
to where, God knows, I came from?

Like a flower with a dead face –
a virgin alone, baptized in holy immolation,

soaking are the petals of my unfulfilled disgrace...
and placed bare, naked is my soul.

My eyes and heart relinquish –
the sullied wine and bitter salts
I passed for the sweetness of the vine

where hate made a friend of love
and the father is a bastard in a cloak.

As the rally bells chime, their stagnant call
for that same want of glory, bereft...

I, being of nature, shy pilgrim,
commit through the pastures of doubt,

past the valleys of the cheat
I crawl head-first with unborn feet,

to find my soul is caged and my truth is frozen;
where next should I drag my ideal?

To the world below, where I shall leave behind
all wretched illusion, my sad ordeal

and become as a Goddess, fallen from the sky
to a place of no return.

The keeper of the gate asked seven times of me
to strip each layer at seven separate doors

to reach the Queen of the Dead, Ereshkigal:
my crown, rings and beads and toggle-pin,

my girdle of shining lights, my bangles
along with the garment of my body were bared,
for such are the rites of a mistress of the Earth.

I become more like stone, as I surrender
each robe around my body,

for when my own time has come,
I shall turn into stone like those immortalized

become, with eyes that show depth
and harbour the deep well that is the abysm,

from punishment
I delved down to sixty strokes of despair;

a prisoner of my own volition
I suffered there, before my brethren star –

Asu-shu-namir – let my heart breathe
and seduced that She-devil with the waters of his life,

before my return made me drink of the same,
and the seven stages of the Goddess were mine to reclaim

and I returned to walk the soil, to Ea's delight –
a daughter of sin determined

I who would give to the Earth, severed from the soil,

through the tunnels deep down into the caves
I became, Ishtar –

She who belongs to the Earth
for the strength of Her flame.

MONOLITH

There are days when my soul listens only
to the hum of stone, held tight
within timeless gulf
under spell
I greet infinity -
this unfathomed divine...
solid to the core
of no human face
your coven speaks your epithet as Truth.

Monolith
I sense the chords of unbroken time.
You could never be my lover
old girl, whatever is your age
deep is the thread
and walk will I along your cold scarp edge,
so eerie is the silence
you would hear the echo...

You are the ore,
Queen of the heap
we minerals blush,
we blossom as grains
ears of the corn
in the grind of a holy quern

where down millennia, fecund beneath
in the roots of the organ,
within the midst of your fabric
your daughters brandish torches
below in subterranean rhythms of rock,
they give you a face
yet they are not you.

They think you are dead mother-rugged...
and yet I know there is more than sad epitaph
between the fractured, broken line of age.

EPITAPH

Embrace me or not...
I am outside the circle,
off the beaten path
glad to be alone,
euphoric I push at the wall:

hidden
wretched
blissful
holy.

A shattering vessel
spilled of my heart's ease
with sleeves rolled
in orgy with my dear friend
cataclysm!

I become everything
and nothing!

And in these transient moments
of violence,
awakenings reap truths
which betray
all the alignment of the stars.

LIQUID

I ponder the mind...
of base thoughts borne of the abyss,
the same clay that grew great beasts,

of creatures crowned wide-winged;
they will rise as far as
I was dragged from the sea...

before my time came
I soared above the isolate heights,
lifting my hope beyond, stretching back

within the far-forgotten psyche
to the murmur of the source
the raging of the shadow

where the boon and the curse
vibrate for supremacy.
This is fluid –

I am the eternal change,
in pursuit of that I cipher...
the mask will frighten from time to time

as much as I know I must kiss
the beauty of my soul; poise balance
in the universe I have made my own.

IMMORTAL

Knelt at the edge of the water cursing his luck,
The downed leaves had fallen like remnants of dust
From the first sun, into the pool of the ascetic.
Waxing the tranquil deadly lake,
That made him a philosopher, bleak as the blue-sky,
Silent as the autumn still, this was day
Pale night has no need for living men
Nor the fulfilled crowns of kings that die like them.

ECSTASY

Under the aegis, enveloped between
The frenzied white wings of ecstasy
Atop the lusty swan in colour of tease
She bade lovers do as lovers please...

EVE

Come close to me, dear, come closer,
betwixt the claws of the tree
In the embrace of rose-fingered dawn,
Before all nature falls, we shall hearken to our own.

Come, first to me in your thoughts. I wait
Below, in regions shown by those most intimate,
Given such power by He that knows His lustful art...
Of lips; caress and eyelash fold
Down in bliss to nourish that which lives within

Come closer. Relish the harmony, Eat of me here.

AMOR

When the eyes that can sing to you
return to me,
I must change nothing,
for the dance around the rose is ours;
truth is with me,
with an embrace, our cord and a knot -
the one which said you did for me.

For I will meet you at roads which cross -
we lovers entangled
in the rivers of our life,
each in the essence of the other
in a ripple
through the tribulation and the trial
where always I return
to the aphrodisia of your eyes,
to hollow beyond to the origin,
that jewel within your darkness.

BELTAIN

Deep is the wood this deathless eve,
for I wish to dance the fire with you,

kiss your sacred copse.
Hand-in-hand, keel o'er

and lie on a bed of bluebells,
wrapping around each other's sphere

immersed in the waters of love,
under the light of the grinning moon

beside the oak and the hawthorn's hearth
and the future we'll walk along the mercury path,

we hasten as lovers of old in this forest of stars,
so deep is the wood this deathless eve,

before all promise fades in the twilight of our time,
so swiftly goes the breeze.

THE DEATH OF ADONIS

I am in love with devils in silks,
they rut like goats
on the hills of singed hope
moaning like infiltrated spirits
into the pulse and smut
of the lusty forest floor
where ploughed is the slavery
out of the bondage,
where I, Adonis, is found at play...

I will swallow the beads of your fluid
devour each petal of your being!

How the fix is found
sweet mistress of my ecstasy...
I am bound, taking of the cup
from the province of your centre,
from which I drink
making glow lush radiance
like minerals spilled upon famished soil -
come flooding river!
I grant you this serpentine tongue
in a boy's unholy grip...

I will sing to you as others have been sung
and on my bed of remembrance
Venus in Her sorrows
will know the depth that could not be,
lest I, Adonis
had not died a mystery...

INCITER

Present then gone,
scattered in the grains
dismembered,
born twice
his drum beats endless.

Drunk down from antiquity
a dithyramb in the fragments
the wild bull is frenzy -
usurping son
to the frontiers come...

The wilderness she waits
lewd glory that dances in groves,
dare dampen the name;
revel among the flutes in the vine
or scattered in the fields
where the drum beats endless on.

MAENAD

I am Paculla Annia...

There was a time in my native Campania
That I was found, lost beneath the daggered moon
Where I heard the rattle of an ancient creed
And I vowed then to frolic dark utters of the truth

I vowed with my fellow daughters of the vine
To haunt the luscious groves in glory
And trust in the canter of wilder hooves
To honour ecstatic the boy God, Bacchus
Lewd in the heat of noon

Whilst a priestess beneath the sun's rays
I honoured the worship of the bull horns over three sacred days
But this was not enough...

So, five sacred nights to satiate each moon,
I made known of rites under dark
Along with strong wine and many a bullock present,
I offered my own sons to orgy
Where maidens frenzied would grind
The sweet flesh of their flower down upon a phallus;
And nature's rage would make man and woman
Equal beneath the stars in caracole

And when the scattered winds delivered us betrayal -
Our cult survived in primal celebration
Never to be curtailed, ever unfinished is the feast...

I am Paculla Annia
I am here and there and everywhere
I am passion, hidden
Priestess, bitch and beast.

SUCCUBUS

Come, O midnight flower.
Over the windowsill
at the haunting hour
in the still dead of night,
when the trees alone
will speak your Sumer tongue

I bade you come, maid Lilith
through the forest as the owl...
your talons will scrape
at the me,

grinding your lost child
into a fountain...

screeching the carnage!
Aboard the wreck of heaven
descending
before you flee
for the wilderness,
shaken from the huluppu tree.

ADORATION

*Much as love's flamed ire is brought to mind
Safer the place is home, here Sappho breathes
Intimacy upon a hearth of smothering song
Made of pearls long thrown from the sky
Mistress unwithered by stroke of time
Despoina, hear my blessed verse...*

SONG-FATHER

No longer do I stand between the worlds
unknown to each abyss.

I am in awe of the wild horns within
the womb of the Great Goddess

and there is more than a mirror
to break that ancient silence;

tapping the pulse I listen
like a blush before the moon,

and I revel in words which become
from words becoming, I am

the lyre, a rose in your hand
the breeze of chords,

I venerate the strings
and as I heave

come the whispers upon the wind.

APHRODITE

Aphrodite - blossom of the ancestral waters
from the beginnings the Earth was your shell...

As the hooves of the salt-sea crashed
you were cast from the sky that screamed
of your violent origin

and your form was born of the foam,
bright daughter of lust and all animate things

from the tumult and the scythe
which severed the first dynasty.

Initiatress to matter; of particles and atoms
and the bodies of all fecund things,
of union, elements and seeds,

you are in us both
when you perform great wonders,

and yet you would trample over the hearth
in your own heart Mistress, I know

this depth that is eternity,
stilled by Time, they say

there is a river in Lesbos that kills stags and maidens
lest they should long for the hearth
and the stone hand of marriage
that even that master of fire could not extinguish
in the longing for so many an Adonis.

With your pearl breasts Cytherean,
your warmth delivers to lustful hearts
and Hera may rise and turn up her nose

but she will need your girdle
and she will wear your myrtle,
for marriage must pay homage
to She that deals in vital promiscuity;

yours is the sap of the spring which fills the flasks of the
dormant Earth
and ignites the chase with the power of desire –

before the rivers begin flow, at the end of the dart's great work.

TO ORPHEUS

The lungs of myth exhale...

they breathe him out
downstream.
wanted to eat him alive
headless
drink his distillation
become his frenzied chorus
pour him through the ages
cast the matter down

flowing down ecstatic,
marking each hour
in wreathes of line -

as if his severed head had sung...

Do not look back Orpheus
the metre is galloping,
three fingers of the dactyl pluck
blessed by the bitches of Bacchus.

The head sang...

song reverberates
and ancient the lyre
it breathes,
carried along
to his priests on the bank -
awaiting the echo -
listening for the wail of the strings.

PERSEPHONE

Deep in the deciduous wood
There is found an odd flower,
And she shines as a beacon
Within the shades for shorter hours.

When winter arrives she turns to progeny
And in metamorphosis, comes struggle...
She scurries into the cracks, between root fingers
Of beech trees that have seen
The universe with their eyes before,
But swiftly passes the day.

For the sap and the wind,
The womb and aery architect
Deliver many a better blessing,
Whilst nature writhes and she screams
Under the emblem of evolving life
So swiftly comes decay, Persephone.

Demeter of the crop, she weeps
And her metaphor 'bove in the swinging stars
Emulates that they give below
In the harsh, cold and still places
Lights, which vital, clash
Their matter and gas with unequal force;

Of motions that will ruin
On pitiful Earth a mother's devotion
For death must be on his way, Persephone.

THE HAG OF LOCH BA

The things that I have seen through all my time
Adam and Eve were young loves, when I was but a girl.
Before the oceans were filled with salt-waves
My beasts roamed wild among the thorny thickets.
Now wiser, I must bathe my old age afore the sun does rise -
My great stature, my apron of stones, my one eye
Dipped in the waters of Loch Ba...
No sound or living lung shall thwart my finer shape
For a Bride's two eyes will be stars in your sky;
My plaits are of the otherworld...
But you must kiss an old crone first; share with me
A bed of lucky clover before you wake, my boy
Offer me your pure heart - this hag
Who'd banged at th'door to sit by your warm fireside
Your kindness I must oblige.

Sit and listen now as the ages seep between us
And touch the summer's turn to the harsh winter hand
You will find me as a stone, a heron or a wolf
Or quiet in a cave come the sun's zenith high
Where quietly, I will whisper my old age.

CIRCE

On the edge of what we know,
a silhouette stands against the moon-crazed sky...

She spares none, dark daughter of the Sun
and needs no more to ponder the end
for she is already there.

No veil attends her mystery,
no man knows where the darkness sets
nor where the dawn thus will rise
yet here, is not far.

As the smoke of her fires raise high,
her beasts drool
dumbstruck to the whim of the sorceress
dumbfounded and tame, she will treat men the same,

the hetaerean's fame now guides the hawk
whose circling movements mock the trap;
tightened is the charmer's noose
around the lost and wandering souls of Illium's war
who'd set sail for home, to a home no more;

soon to be cast to a sty with a swift wand's work
from skin and speech to bristle and grunt –

Circe – witch and weaver of all
who fall under her dominion.

She that lured with siren's song
to entrance with wine and fine food
missed one fool, a fool yet duped
and escape he made to the waiting ships –
bound for his captain, Odysseus...

On his return to Circe's lair, his sword remained
unsheathed, even as Hermes –
the wing-footed one - drew nigh to the front of his path,
to warn him of the ways of the island's villainess,

and the messenger gave him the drops of the moly,
potion and shield to Circe's own designs,
told him he must make her swear by all Her power
that she would do him no harm,
for even a man who lays with the witch
would soon find his own shortcoming and end...

And yet the tale bends with the hero appeased
by the mistress who gave him three sons
and a year that pleased Odysseus.

And his freed men, of their own volition
sated their desires and drank the heady wines,
they devoured all delights of Aeaea's frontier
under the spell of the Queen.

In later times, borne perhaps of the legend's omen,
men and ships would skirt the Isle,
hearing less fortunate cries where Circe may still ply her tricks
upon
any unwitting eye, seduced by the lethal fog which sillies the
mind,
for lust can be cruel and lust may be blind
but Circe ever opens her doorway
to the world that dwells below.

DREAM

To wander for the dark bridge:
I have been of the dawn
and have passed into dusk
in the night-worn hours.

I cross the river
Alea iacta est
into vaster stream,
this place of origin -
first Kingdom of Man is a dream.

THE END

47

www.ingramcontent.com/pod-product-compliance
Lightning Source LLC
Chambersburg PA
CBHW071757080526
44588CB00013B/2281